THIRD WISH WASTED

Roddy Lumsden's first book *Yeah Yeah Yeah* (1997) was shortlisted for Forward and Saltire prizes. His second collection *The Book of Love* (2000), a Poetry Book Society Choice, was shortlisted for the T.S. Eliot Prize. *Mischief Night: New & Selected Poems* (Bloodaxe Books, 2004) was a Poetry Book Society Recommendation. *Third Wish Wasted* (Bloodaxe Books, 2009) is his latest collection.

He is a freelance writer, specialising in quizzes and word puzzles, and has held several residencies, including ones with the City of Aberdeen, St Andrews Bay Hotel, and as "poet-in-residence" to the music industry when he co-wrote *The Message*, a book on poetry and pop music (Poetry Society, 1999). His other books include *Vitamin Q: a temple of trivia, lists and curious words* (Chambers Harrap, 2004). His anthology *Identity Parade: new British and Irish poets* is due from Bloodaxe Books in 2010. Born in St Andrews, he lived in Edinburgh before moving to London.

RODDY LUMSDEN

Third Wish Wasted

BLOODAXE BOOKS

ISBN: 978 1 85224 828 4

First published 2009 by
Bloodaxe Books Ltd,
Highgreen,
Tarset,
Northumberland NE48 1RP.

www.bloodaxebooks.com
For further information about Bloodaxe titles
please visit our website or write to
the above address for a catalogue.

Bloodaxe Books Ltd acknowledges
the financial assistance of
Arts Council England, North East.

Cover design: Neil Astley & Pamela Robertson-Pearce.

Printed in Great Britain by
Bell & Bain Limited, Glasgow, Scotland.

with love to NJB and CPB

ACKNOWLEDGEMENTS

Acknowledgements are due to the following publications and websites where some of the poems were published: *Fulcrum*, *The London Magazine*, *Magma*, *The Oxonian Review of Books*, *Poetcasting*, *Poetry London*, *Poetry Review*, *Rising*, *Showcase* (at www.laurahird.com), *The Shuffle Anthology*, *Snakeskin*, *South Bank Poetry* and *Trespass*.

Particular gratitude to the editors of *Poetry* in Chicago who published thirteen of these poems and to Andy Ching who published seven of the poems here in the pocket book *Super Try Again* (Donut Press 2007). 'A Transatlantic Creed' was written for the wedding of Clare Sandercock and Jamie Doornbos. 'An English Village' was commissioned by the British Film Institute for an event promoting their Mediatheque archive. 'Bloom' and 'To the End of the Day' were written as part of a commission from SHOWstudio (www. showstudio.com) to write new work during a fashion shoot with photographer Nick Knight and model Kate Moss.

Hearty thanks to A.B. Jackson and Ahren Warner for their helpful advice on the manuscript, and to Nina Blackett for her advice, love and support.

CONTENTS

The Young

You bastards! It's all sherbet, and folly
makes you laugh like mules. Chances
dance off your wrists, each day ready,

sprites in your bones and spite not yet
swollen, not yet set. You gather handful
after miracle handful, seeing straight,

reaching the lighthouse in record time,
pockets brim with scimitar things. Now
is not a pinpoint but a sprawling realm.

Bewilderment and thrill are whip-quick
twins, carried on your backs, each vow
new to touch and each mistake a broken

biscuit. I was you. Sea robber boarding
the won galleon. Roaring trees. Machine
without levers, easy in bowel and lung.

One cartwheel over the quicksand curve
of Tuesday to Tuesday and you're gone,
summering, a ship on the farthest wave.

Liminal

To the avocet, delicate, a whim
with fixtures, pitched in shingle,
not quite stomping, the universe is
a belly of twilit mud, an accordance

of ripples, a vouchsafe of shoreline;
his reflection is companion enough
and with his sharp canticle he pledges
himself to the clarion evening.

Against Complaint

Though the amaryllis sags and spills
so do those my wishes serve, all along the town.
And yes, the new moon, kinked there in night's patch,
tugs me so – yet I can't reach to right the slant.
And though our cat pads past without a tail, some
with slinking tails peer one-eyed at the dawn, some
with eyes are clawless, some with sparking claws
contain no voice with which to sing
of foxes gassing in the lane.
      Round-shouldered pals
parade smart shirts, while my broad back supports
a scrubby jumper, fawn or taupe.
      The balding English
air their stubble, while some headless hero sports
a feathered hat. I know a man whose thoroughbred
grazes in his porch for want of livery.
There are scholars of Kant who can't find Kent
on the map, and men of Kent who cannot
fathom Kant.
    We who would polish off a feast have lain
late in our beds, our bellies groaning, throats on fire.
We who'd drain a vat of wine have drunk
our own blood for its sting.
      Each of us in tatters flaunts
one treasured garment flapping in the wind.

How the Champion Sleeps

No lamp roars, and the ashen seasons
anchor, nine miles off. Mice numb
to neat and silver statues in the floorboards.

New darkness folds itself around
each bed-leg, makes treasure of the night
and wads the creak of light below the door.

Don't try to count the years we wished
to be dreamless, as he is, to catalogue
the sullen evenings wasted, roosting

from foot to foot, turning in a mash
of psyche and sweat. His shirt and coat sit
crisp on a chair-back. All candles

stiff to touch, the skylight black and bells
throughout the house are stifled, and if one
was struck, its chilling song would chase

through rooms yet fall short. Stepping in
behind his eyes, you'd recognise the dark,
familiar from your heyday, which is gone.

Middleton

Twinned with Chandigarh (India), Port Augusta (Australia), Juarez (Mexico), Bo (Sierra Leone), Winnipeg (Canada), Middlesbrough (UK), Sialkot (Pakistan), Magadan (Russia)

The morning pans in black and white
     on mass retail developments,
industrial gulleys at the town edge,
     refineries marked on maps as palaces,
passers-through, who are the majority,
     rolling up their windows against
fish-scented air and hissing machinery,

here, where time is tossed from hand
     to hand until you stumble and slump,
where drunken gun mechanics linger,
     dozing on the landfill, and layers
of silt coat and choke the concrete parks
     where feral girls kick and count
the looted goods, their first grey hairs,

where a five year old gives you the finger
     from a kerb on President's Road
where he sells a thin newspaper which touts
     the jeopardies and mispers,
and that's not evening settling on the tracks
     but a daily implosion, surefooted decline,
the purest essence of despair, life tax

for the settlers – can't call them residents –
     who watch the spewing smokestacks
beyond the inching black river through glass
     which shivers and cracks, who whisper
beneath low ceilings in twiny accents
     in the rainy, lifelong comedown
while blackflies the size of house-cats,

death pilots, circle their pale scalps.

Wetness as Motive Concept

Honoured figures of dust and doubt
hold their hands above the flames
and hold, since we must know the ways
of water, which is only wet
when fingers are thrust into it;
I hardly ever know these days
and rarely have I made such games
but when the rain brings, rain brings rout.

A Transatlantic Creed

(an epithalamium)

Belief in the great crossings, wings treading
a glacial sky, a tail feather tumbling
a mile and a half.

Believe the horizon is yours to march upon,
your own dear wish, drawn divine
from ice-cliff to surf-beach.

Belief in deep code swishing in a twist
of wire, a mint glitch of light,
an all-night stare.

Believe that there are answers, across
and down, that you will wake to,
vivid and imperial.

Belief in a voice carried across the squares
of gardens, the shunting speed of sound,
the lilt and still of it.

Believe in the clinch – when two make one
the glassy rings of fear slip off
and clatter in corners.

Belief in the landing stage, jade shallows,
the pouncing third wave out, swell,
abyssal warmth.

Believe in might and will, the shaded street ends
where hands meet. One journey done, one
charted and started on.

DPD

A place of some power, this back-way corridor:
a tile run where my amateur camera sets up
its amygdala dolly zoom, one life spooling,
my low-spectrum screen idol throwing shapes,
becoming part of the process, of the pattern.

Another room of power where I lock the door:
white-tiled walls, red-tiled floor and a *skylight*:
just that one word gifting me a pleasant quease
like the curiosity that chums the plateau phase,
the brain and the body rattling well together.

And a chair of power from which I tally ways
or scan the knots in wood, unweighing damage,
chasing diagonals in a twelve by twelve display
of anything, when picture is no longer image
but colour, number, hunger, my life no more

a gaudy story being told, but wondrous blur.

Maximising the Audience

Not enough to imagine you all naked

so I picture you as sand eels in the shallows

I daydream you as babies waggling mittens

I conjure you as spokes on an old wheel

and reconjure you as arrows in a quiver

I envisage you as knots on barbed wire

as a horde of ghosts waltzing in a barn

I picture you as bandits romping into town

as daisies round the bandstand, blades of sedge:

you look astounding – I can see it now.

Taste

They say that to look at a lemon
is to taste a lemon.

Even to think of a lemon
will make your mouth bloom

with the breeze and tang of the groves.
Just a sideways glimpse

and your tongue runs tart.
Someone in a back room

in Bangkok mentions one
and your cheeks meet.

Until you lap the lemon long and deep
you will not have this art.

A Story of Spice

Since we are human and we seek
what is beyond the ear, behind
the yard's back wall, all that lies

outside our giddy orbis, we have sent
caravels and coracles and caravans
across tasky seas of sand or salt,

slow-blooming enterprise, our coins
thrown into such wells, our wishes
bright against a sullen sky

and have surrendered one in five
(a thumb lopped off) to pools of fire,
to brawling clans who came our way

as we went theirs, and all to bring
the scorch and tang in sacks and jars
with which our cooks will bind and brim

the evening air, while men draw ale
and women dance and children run
through golden fields to golden homes.

Warnerian

Westminster Bridge Road   the day is your enemy
until you prove otherwise   and it has hung
a swing   one wooden block   two hairy ropes
from a bent tree   and set down a mangled toaster
its plugless flex   not leading to a reason
for this tableau vivant   of a Kindertotenmalen
lost to the great galleries

      I'm stung by the visual
hoist up and out   of the comfort of listenage
the unsinge of advice   unlace your boots
before you kick them off   never buy a wine
available by the glass   or offer custom
where dress codes flourish

      Sift gisting advantage
from disadvantage   from the -ish   the -esque of
the moment your skepsis   becomes your sepsis

The Microkite

The quarter horse still isn't ready to be backed.
There's talk of new flooring for the upstairs rooms,
a mention of a sofa-bed for visitors.

The quiz team tell me I'm looking healthy:
half a stone dropped, a shave, a ten-minute haircut.
It's the first time they've seen my ears.

London is greyer this spring than it was in winter.
I'm still moping on my stolen doctor's bag
dumped in a skip somewhere off Charing Cross Road.

In the din of a low-ceilinged restaurant, voices gurge
till the left side of my head begins to fizz.
I right myself. The anchovies sing and fly with salt.

There are answers to all things, even that old man
on Westminster Bridge whose fishing line
looped upward till the crowd lost sight of it.

My grandfather lost his hearing early on
and family history is cloudy as to whether it was
the noise of the Great War or Ménière's disease.

When he was relieved, he saw his brother
among the reinforcements – last time they met –
which is especially different to Eric and myself

meeting by the quiz machine in The Wellington.
You so rarely meet people by chance in the city:
some people record such events in their diaries.

We've taken to drinking wine, for different reasons.
When the question comes up about which city
Beethoven died in, I press A without a thought.

Early Night

I'm off to bed soon, and won't see
the end of this, so fill me in:
does the kitten escape from the tumble drier?
Will the old sawmill ever re-open
after what happened there?
Do the students ever reach the spelling bee
in Cottonwood, or does the stormcloud stay
above their Dodge, the rabid Great Dane lapping
at the windscreen?
                        That lazy girl
with a stream of blood down her cheek –
does she risk it, will she take flight
or tremble where she is?
And if I wake, and there she is, sleeping,
the pillow streaked, the bomber jacket
stained with leaf mould round her shoulders,
will I have the words to drag her back
or will the planet stutter,
hanging helpless in the sights
of one great laser, the countdown dropping?

Flashpoints

Must have been sparks from a passing train, or a little darling
with a lighted paper
— OVERHEARD IN A TRAIN STOPPED DUE TO A TRACKSIDE FIRE

— feathers and fine dust settle on coils — grassland spinning under powerlines — punky logs, duff wood and a skyful of lightning — those downed cables chant — sudden schism in a panel box, wire candling — coals knock through the rusted brazier — fine dead fuel crisping in a clearing — two flints tocked together — nuthusks in an ashtray, kicked over — lithium leaping out of oil — teenage weather — lino blistering under a lazy stove — the laser straying — electrics snarling in an unmanned sub-station — solar waste docking in heavy slash — creeping fever — corpse candles licking the yews — a ruck of oily rags huffs into flame — a fire whirlwind rips from culm bank to conifer stand — the sun's hand reaches through an ice lens — the tea light slips — a tipped lamp — a deal struck and stoked by malice and accelerant — thinners and primus meeting secretly — stiving fumes in a flue pipe — the footlight fomenting the stage drape — firedamp blues the marsh — campfire embers lurk under ashes — short distance spotting in juniper and oak — the pan boiled dry and the tray on the hob — a butt drops through a floorboard — a turbine blade shears — brush and debris gallop into colour — a firebrand kicked across a barn floor — the fired hand creeps back into the curing shed — blowtorch, cutting torch, touchpaper, grease slosh — the bow and drill is kindling its song — the Joshua tree biding its end time —

Fuegos Artificiales

Boys swilling in the cactus pits, whose tongues
are swollen ovals, beguiled by fire; the race is on

to reach the devil: haywire, mayhem, high wires
where masked girls pad; pale flares

of firefly green and scarlet spill
up sombre trails where sky makes way; dark hills

shake beneath a curse; that Jesus walks tonight
you wouldn't guess; far earthlights chime;

from here the roads course east where scorched rocks
ring and young stars drift on beach tracks:

spirit wrestlers who know the sea, drunken runners
who risk the hiss and sting of bonfires,

all who dare the heaving night where rockets surge
and plummet, spin to rags beneath the surf.

Keepsakes

Having failed for a third time to witness
the sight of sights – the sun
rising over the city of sand –

I took off due west from Tierra del Fuego
in an unmarked plane
and flew until I found dry land

which meant Tierra del Fuego, and lay
in a wind-tossed dune
where I could never grow tanned

and no one could see your name tattooed
in ink the colour of skin
or the lock of hair snuck in my hand.

Springheel Jack

Will we ever visit his land of pitch and ice,
who called to our daughters from the gate
and spirited fire, who tore across our rooftops
in impossible boots, his oilskin capes
glowing as he sprang from spire to gable-end,

with steely fingers, scratching at the bellies
of long girls smoking in lanes behind terraces,
lighting his way by blowing white-hot flame,
whose spring-prints in the snow were boltholes
to drop through into cold and peaceful hell?

Cute

Before the sky shook loose that night
and the snow came, this terrible word

had passed my lips two times: first
when we saw a snail nosing along the lip

of the car-park. *Cute!* I clipped it
with my Chinese leather slip-on

then tapped again, the way a brother
would snap the obedient silence

in the monastery refectory by cracking
the top of a goose egg. *Don't*, you said,

not knowing this is how slugs are made,
set free from their jails. And later,

seeing the words *Shadow Boxer*
felt-tipped on the Gentlemen's wall,

I surrendered again that mellifluous bullet
of a word to the world. *Cute!* I thought,

a shadow boxer and a giant of graffiti
to boot, and showed the empty loo

my thumbs up, considering him, inky,
a quiet champion on a stained duvet,

punching towards the ceiling,
throwing shapes onto the mustard wall,

punching up at the snowy roof,
his mother snoring in the next room.

Postcoital

The screen flips into haze
or sunders to a glyph.
         It's hard to tell.

We lie like walruses in oil
or salt drops in a swell.
         Well, who can say?

Just then you whisper
calling me *cherub*, or *roué*.
         I'm not sure which.

Outside, Scotland, or is it England,
rearing in the last light?
         I can never decide.

Shoreline Charismatic

I have seen the sea-edge
        ambassador to stars
                gathering and greeting
and the track to the sea
        zedding north through gorse
                compass-constant
but since each night
        I am fetched into
                the grasp of sleep
I have never seen
        the blackthorn draw forth
                needles from the branch
that they might stitch
        each salted drop
                – the sea itself –
each miracle blink of
        viscous metal, lulling gases
                liquid grace

Between the Penny Dropping and the Penny Landing

The things we want most we will never have.

We learned this when we overheard the song
of a slant moon which wraps the land below,
which courts significance in every corner,
spreads the blueshift, ekes the silver rose

and finds the coin, mid-fall, which will decide
the night for us: the half-chance sounding lower
than a cat step or a spinning leaf or raindrops
meeting on a skylight. Moonlight hones

the bidden street. While the penny spins,
pale beams catch on a lost key in a nest,
roll over roofs and drop into the alley,
and we are shadows in that alley. Only

when I used up all my nos did I say yes.

Contagious Light

That I didn't speak in those times:
the pier spilling out into the sea,
a half-love spilling under me,
the weather saying '70 or '91;

that the train met buffers in towns
my fondest touch ignored,
so little did I need to need that world,
my sorry calculations done;

that a grand parade of light teems
heatless, sacks and sets fire
to chanced-on minor cities of desire
proves all and none.

Hunter's Stew

(after Mickiewicz)

In every pan and kettle, stew gurgles
and pundits and poets circle
with half-boiled testaments, blind stabs
to nail its marvel smell, its omen stain,
its dab-hand tricking on the lips.

Mere persuasions, diagnoses,
molly words can't catch its essence.
Not for the mouths of pale city wretches,
only those with lust in the singing voice
can taste it, those who know the shades

in the byways, who've cantered homeward,
sore, with the catch on their shoulders.
This is no weekday bubble-up, and not
your canteen casserole, this hunter's stew
squares up to you and grants you wishes.

New-lugged from the earth, cabbage
is the heart of the alchemy, sluiced and sliced,
tart and zesty, snaking in the pot,
welcoming with wanton arms choice collops
and cantles of gammon and game.

As scullions and skivvies gather and gaze,
flushed to the cheeks, dabbing their temples,
the mishmash seethes, the geyser threatens
to blow, froth leaping at the pot's lip
lacing the air and flavouring the hour.

Be ready. Buff your arsenal of spoons,
give up your chases, charge your bowls
with the spoils of the cosmos. Ah, be brave.
Push through the hot fog to the stove
and make the copper kettles clang

and hide the stuff, let's see you yell
and yank it down – watch it disappear
like spring ice, like camphor, banished
to the dark within you, to the gullet's gloom,
the Stygian belly, the tarry, singing gut.

And peer through the steam, to see the pots
now scraped and scuppered, the cooks
glutted and dozing, with ladles in hand,
like lesser fire gods, guarding the core
of a smoking and sacred volcano.

Jackpot

The season's triumphs – still
     and brackish water gleaming,
the log-stack at the wood's core,

     a rusky pony blissing
in the early dusk, as hammerflush
     dances from the anvil;

the owl moans through late sun haze
     and the barnyard reels
with shadowy dens for hiding in.

     Glimpsed at a window,
past sifting peat smoke, a brisk girl
     near calm, known to us all.

That the depths beneath the bridge
     are cold and cruel
is not in question, though no one yet

     will venture a name for
this stout boy striding out
     whose fate it is to plunge

into the mile-deep pool
     and rope the great bell, lost to us
these thousand years.

Affinity

My gaze has chased you over ponds, affinity,
      through silver stations, the mesh fences
            parting pastures, orange quells and orchards

to limits where no alarm bell will waken
      those uncharged with duty, fuss or hurry:
            a beetle drift toward the region undecreed,

the lands towards the boundary undreamt,
      where running streams are falling pistol fair,
            affinity, and grass fields in unwedded blush

call birds down to hurrah bleak hours
      and if we meet by evening's tilt, we should
            send down the night, surrender to the edge.

Beyond Pale

None more blonde
than those travel agents spilling out
onto The Strand,
not the Finnish netball league,
or peroxidised disco belles,
the ash-smearing hermitess
or square one hydrogen,
beckoning from its dazzle.

We caught wind
of a wind that had been caught,
yellower than fire, but not that.
And not the sand cat, the albino camel,
nor Spanish lace or Rhenish wine.
From time to time, reports
creep through of a cadmium ship
or a fine pearl gumdrop
but none will do.

No matter how the others flash
their flaxen souls,
their citrine eyes, they will not win,
though each
resorts to platinum and bleach
and strands of ivory.
For those travel agents *are* the ones
you are after: none, *none*
were ever blonder.
That's your answer.

September

A thin song sounding
from the Meeting House.

All the wasted fever
and now summer ending.

Last sun sifts the last vowel
of Tranquil Vale.

The heath dark in abandon;
one sour voice.

He whose kite flew highest
must do most winding.

Clichés of Time-lapse

The mushroom billows from loam,
nosing upward from a whit
then foaming back to grievance;

horned snails career in almost circles;
a crow shrugs off its sooty coat,
jigs and sighs down to a skeleton;

Ayers Rock wades through the red end
of the paintbox; pleasure boats zip
to and by from the calm of the quay;

nimbostratus patrols a plain;
daybreak, noon and small hours watch
the dab and weave of cabs on Lexington.

Stone Tape Theory

Whosoever has pushed a tear of bread
into a glossy pool of gravy
has entered history

paying the ticket price, playing statues
as they lift to their mouths
a fine brine of self,

striking the figures of those minor gods
who light the mineral tapes
of creek and cliff:

the shirtless walker raising his palm
to close out the sun's clamour
or some castaway

fetching up the cold gush to her lips
as she hangs at the stream
and a dawn hunter

dipping his thumb in a kicking breeze
to taste the *is, are, am,*
to prove the future.

The Beautiful

Into perplexity: as an itch chased round
an oxter or early man in the cave mouth
watching rain-drifts pour from beyond

his understanding. Whether to admire
the mere sensation, enough, or hold out
for sweeter ornament, vessels of wonder

born with that ur-charm of symmetry;
lovely ones we ache to prize and praise,
climb into and become because they try

our day-by-day significance: some of us
ugly and most of us plain, walked past
in the drowned streets: pearls of paste,

salted butter, secondary colours. They
drift unapproached, gazed never-selves,
blunt paragons of genetic industry. We

desire them but cannot want such order.
We stand, mouths open, and cannot help
stammering our secrets, nailed to water.

–

Sammy's Noodle House & Grill

What did you order?

The soup with won tons, char sui and duck. The short ribs with black beans. A steam-tin of the pork-shrimp shui mai.

And what was good?

Beakers of ice-water the waiters kept filling. The fulminous tea, the dizzying broth. The dim sum. The bullion of ribs rolled along tongue and tooth. The slight bite to the beans.

What disappointed?

The sour breath of my neighbour's English broccoli. And the duck, but the duck always does with its coop tang and inch of fat.

What was the weather?

Slow flakes slanted on the West Village. Easter Sunday.

And who was your companion?

The fine wool overcoat of the man at the next table was draped on the seat opposite me.

How was the matter resolved?

With empty plates and partly empty plates and a residue of ice and my neighbours nodding and bowing and gone and the waiters going and coming and napkins and dollars and solace and a grin against the snipping wind from the South.

Will the world end in the lifetimes of our children?

I can't say. Not for sure.

Angels Hurled Down

An Easter parade. First you hear it –
        woodwind from lisping speakers –

then you glimpse it along a side street
        and you long to *feel* that rapture

yet instead fists tighten as you stop
        on Union Square; a bitter wind whips

your thinning hair, you watch the majorettes
        glad-hand the day in yellow suits

and weather too unwholesomely crisp
        for pompoms and thighs; most

daydream of chocolate eggs or blister pads
        and boy bands, though one perhaps

shares your desire for a wrinkled, risen Christ
        swimming into the harbour.

And yes, that is blood in the water.
        What else would it be?

Tandem

I have never known happiness
though I have seen it blink
in the sun-stretched city;

as I crossed New York Harbor
I watched another ferry
headed inward, where one boy,

one girl, lifted by it, jumped
in tandem as if on a trampoline,
sparky as the wake behind

and once at Berlin Zoo,
a beatifical hyena, swollen with it –
twice her own size,

days away from dropping
her sprawl of cubs – at whom
I stared rapt until I saw

she was not looking out of *her* cage
but into mine; and that
I'd held these bars all my life.

From a Motel 6

Things to carry with you always:
a bad book, a bottle opener, a mind
as open as it can be, at your age.

The bad book's to ease you, trouble
dusted off, you rarely turn a page,
scanning again an entry on

the history of the popsicle
or how porcupines mate, the TV
still on low, the same ads for meds,

same maps of the Eastern seaboard
where more rain will fall today
than any April day on record.

Hours yet till they'll clear the schedule
for the latest college kill spree;
you turn beneath thin sheets.

The opener's for the bottles
of Fat Tire Amber, warm in your case,
(clinking up against your Joint

& Cartilage Formula – twice the price
at home), warm and frothing
in a plastic cup, tasting heaven-sent

but from Fort Collins, voted Best Place
to Live last year. The open mind's
a wooden wheel to grip, a thing

to steer love, guns, the usual ends,
only the weather stands above us,
toiling, as it relishes to do.

The book lies open. In twenty hours,
back in Manhattan, you'll stand
on Broadway with the master poet

who offers tea and talk, politely,
but you can see he's tired,
thinking of his flooded house

and so you slip into the wired
evening shift, drift east and south,
disappear into the nightly

warp and weft on puddled avenues
and cross streets – to Ace Bar on 5th
with two pin tables: *Family Guy*

and *Pirates of the Caribbean* – buy
a Fire Rock Pale and change a five
for quarters. Tonight, the lanes and loops

will take easy, swallow shots, flippers
supple as your own thick fingers
(meaning not quite factory new),

you will shoot the ball up to the ship
a seventh time – REPLAY! flashes –
sending scads of pirates to the deep.

Ludlow

An inch from the curse and pearled
by the evening heat   I shake
my polo-neck and a cool draught
buffs my chest. What rises is
my animal aroma   the scent
of blue ribbon stock   the sort
a starred chef would ladle from
a zinc-bottomed pan   to soften
and savour the hock he has sawn
and roasted for the diners out front
who sip at shots of pastis and gnaw
around the pits of kalamata olives.
                              My head
sits in his fridge: stooping for herb
butter, our eyes meet and he touches
my cotton-cold face   just as once
I stroked your cheek in a dream
you suffered in a room above the river.

Self Portrait as Hard Work

Tricky work sometimes not to smell yourself,
ferment being constant – *constant as carnival sweat*
(a non-stock phrase I palmed from a girl from Canada,
a land where I once saw this graffiti: LIFE IS GREAT).

And I have tasted myself, especially when I spilled
sinigang all down my arm in a Pinoy workers' caff
in Little Manila. I drank sinigang (is soup drunk?)
in Big Manila too, with all its dead skyscrapers.

Seen myself? In looking glasses or, looking down,
stocky as a shift working cop, maybe a Mexican cop
full of beans (frijoles, I mean, not vim), paunch full
of sopa de vigilia, pulling over a sozzled bus driver.

Heard myself speak fluently in my own language,
have heard myself too described as hard work
(as hard to get through as Scotch broth), though once
someone rather bladdered told me I was magnetic.

And I may as well admit that I have touched myself
(who hasn't?). In a forest, on a train, in New York
and Paris with unparalleled handiwork, sinning
as I go, merry as an office boy spooning onion soup.

Season of Quite

With refreshments and some modesty and home-drawn maps,
the ladies of the parish are marshalling the plans in hand,
devising the occasions, in softest pencil: the Day of Hearsay,
Leeway Week, the Maybe Pageant, a hustings on the word
nearby. Half-promised rain roosts in some clouds a mile out,
gradual weather making gradual notes on the green, the well,
the monument, the mayor's yard where dogs purr on elastic.

Everything taken by the smooth handle then, or about to be,
hiatus sharp in humble fashion. A small boy spins one wheel
of an upturned bike, the pond rises, full of skimmed stones
on somehow days, not Spring, not Summer yet. Engagements
are announced in the *Chronicle*, a nine yard putt falls short.
Dark cattle amble on the angles of Flat Field. The ladies close
their plotting books and fill pink teacups, there or thereabouts.

An English Village

What you visit is not what we are
who hold the words of songs to sway to
who satisfy the cracks in ponds
who strike a match in many ways
who make a mansion of a shelter
who call rain by its given names
who talk through what we have to chew
who sit on roofs as evenings melt
who track the halfways through each yard
who know the weights our heads can take
who balance on the tails of carts
who answer to each toll of bells
who point the way to mooring stones
who higgle, carry, yoke and chap
who hear the barn sing under storm
who keep the pugmill stirring on
who stand among the tansy itching
who buy worlds from the ballad seller
who news and bicker round the pump
who set a fire to know a fire
who run beasts down the hidden roads
who thresh and glean and stack then dance
who roast an ox at each new king

On an Old Scots Dictionary

Crack the tartan spine, flick through, you'll find
at least as many terms for slut and slattern

as there are for crops and farming implements:
clort and *clatch*, *latheron*, *soss* and *slodge* explained

as 'lumpish sloven', 'plate-licker', 'a strumpet',
'a heavy drab', 'a slobbering woman of low morals';

so many words that I picture her wide-thighed
in a loft of the barn and her wild hair's in the straw,

ill-defined, and if I can't see her eyes, how can I
find them in the throngs and queues: the herring girls

newsing on the quay head, high-haired bathing belles
in lines at Largs, the lunch-hour temps on Rose Street.

Farringdon

Call me when your new friends bore you,
when flags no longer hoist themselves above
your diamond brilliance
like you were someone.

If sleazy tarmac grips your heels,
harsh maybes rise or sirens squall, think me,
whatever stroke of day
on Holborn Viaduct.

Now roll there in your eyrie flat:
now sofa bed, now bathroom floor, now bed,
the songs of Saffron Hill
infecting you.

Your champagne's done, and honeyed ham
with speckled beans. Not sharing isn't done.
Your reading lamp gleams on,
my book thrown down.

Now force my image. Let me loose,
girl overboard, to spike your faith: untamed,
intent that you might wake
and be someone.

In Liberace's Memory

First comes love... Because you knew the backroom boys
keep the chains oiled, the theatre secretary keeps the boss

in line, the doorman sees to the little things that matter,
you learned their names, asked after kids and mothers,

remembered that Larry who drew up contracts in Boston
shared your taste for iced buns, that Heidelmann's assistant

was Shula and not Sheila and stored all this information
there beneath your perfect bouffant, in perfect fashion.

Old Kittenish on the Keys, they called you, while *Whisper*
magazine claimed all your hormones were in your fingers,

fingers that made you a half-decent mid-West Paderewski,
an eighty-eight key, two thousand tune jukebox all ready

inside your marcelled mind, and room still for flashbacks
of all those muscled tricks, the Hilton, custom grands, rocks

dripping from a silk three-piece, skinflicks, the Phantom
5 silver Rolls Royce you had shipped back from London

where The Queen requested to touch your 'virgin fox'
fur train and watched you showboat from the royal box;

everywhere you made it – and everywhere you made it
into: the motor-homes and jump-rope songs, *Top Secret*,

Hush and *Private Lives*, the pick-up trucks of Mexicans
you cruised in parking lots, a top at the top, the American

dream you dreamed in piano-shaped beds, of chandeliers
and chauffeurs, cascades of toy dogs down velveteen stairs,

and every year a Vegas year, from the rhinestone footlights
of the Pabst Theatre, Milwaukee-famous, to late headlights

frisking Camellia Street and Valley Vista Boulevard
glistening. You never did forget yourself – not one word.

Ornithogalum Dubium

Lame again, I limp home along Lawn Terrace
with a flowering sun star in a paper wrap

then back to the village with a lame cat
twisting and woeful in her cage.

Bread these days isn't baked to last:
how sad those posh loaves thudding off

in pine breadbins all around the Heath:
soulless latter-day pets, frisky for a day

or two, then binned or thrown to foxes,
off loaves just a sip of gloom below

the caged birds you would once have found
in the parlours of those same mansions,

lone canaries dinking their mirrors,
dipping once in a while for a sip of milk.

Lover's Leap

Blue black, constant night in the thick of
the narrow head; the cream of the bones
or quick malachite of an eye to sigh for,
upstream, the child's first surge of lust;

a slow pink in the palm; the red brick of
the sleeping-house in stasis at the loan's
sun-fed end; silver or its leaping cipher
from sea to bar to weir to dam, to dust.

The Hook

As you will doubtless know, and as I understand,
most men think of sex a hundred times a day.
For him, it was just once, but it was always *her*:
that first time, when he had hooked a finger
around her pearls and drawn her in toward him,
thumbing open the collar of her blue blouse.

He never got to the second button, for
the moment stalled when things rose in the ether
and colonised his mind: crumbs on a tray,
sailors calling in the doorway of Jubilee House;
a bull roaring glory on the last of the land
or the sleeve of night tightening around him.

Dying Horse, Tyssen Road

How still he is and coarse
      with florin eyes.
The paving stones roll under him;
      hooves dab the gutter.

I have touched at many doors,
      claimed them home,
known the bull's blood, penny toffee
      taste of London Pride.

When I crouch there to smooth
      his throbbing ribs
my hand sinks through the cage,
      meets tar and grit.

Side street becomes again farm track
      where lupins climb;
when dawn lifts, a frisking colt
      stamps beside me.

Against Conceit

Don't say *Sir Pigeon in his cobalt bonnet*,
          don't find among your notes
jottings on duvets and blizzards and the page

unwalked across   *black missives of girlhood*
must be sent off   and do not claim the furnace
of the universe is powered by human screams.

When the dark turns dark   or when
          the bullet lifts a scalp
it is enough to know the lover feels the slap

that the world can hear the sharp shout
which wakes the cat   her claws
one inch from the rabbit's bobbing scut.

Sea Air

Because we were a pair and dined alone
outside the bistro on the harbour lip,
they tried to serve us *fruits de mer*
we hadn't ordered, the bullish waiter
setting down steaming coquilles, crab claws,
some sort of lobe in a plague of bubbling cheese;
I waved him on, too late, and a child appeared
and lit a fizzing lantern at the table edge.

We were already full: the house broth
was a well of clots and shreds – already full
and cousins, not the spoons they took us for:
that winking child, the woman who waltzed by
and frisked us with her Jesus roses
and the waiter whose eye I tried to catch,
my features garbled in some manly code
that stood for *cousins*, gazing an anti-gaze,

betokening our small talk, in-town-tonight
family catch-up, hinting at dull seasons
we spent as children: while adults chased drinks
in two-tone lounges, we tumbled for yahtzees,
teasing out jack straws, lobbing a wet sponge
into a pail, a tournament we saw through
with lukewarm relish. *Sea air*, they say,
will do you good, a twist of peril,

a briny flux to quibble in the lungs,
the bronchioles pulsing, but *never try
to drink the sea* – now, which language is that
a proverb from? And so I closed my eyes,
reopened them on the woman she wears now
upon the girl she was. Schemes lost to chance,
days broken by persuasions, anomie
in full bloom – what haven't I been prey to?

While she talked work, I was falling lost
in some indulgent fog, dire reverie:
why couldn't I want her – what switch is flicked,
which limbic valve screwed tight? A beacon blinked
a mile along the coast road, the coffee tasted
of coffee and we left the chocolate mints
on their floral saucer. Yacht ropes slapped
in rising wind, she hauled into her coat,

the waiter bent to blow the lamp. I waved
her into a taxi for her five miles home
and padded past the shutting harbour bars
where barmen barely old enough to drink
were bottling up and stacking chairs, towards
the guest house I'd politely booked, Yale locks,
a groaning staircase and a bed with sheets
where later I would burst back from a dream

of teasing out her bones like spillikins.
White curtains flipped, a dark wardrobe loomed.
You never dream the bones of one you love.
And yet I lay there in the almost quiet
counting through the bones of the body:
two hundred and six of them, I knew,
counting, from the oar in the thigh
to the charms floating in her middle ear.

Great Beauties and Where to Place Them on the Stage

Carolina at the lacquered upright,
limbered fingers set to play
the black keys only;

Emma, where her shadow dims
the rake, the bombshell news
primed in her mouth;

Constanza in her wedding outfit
underneath a bust of Juno,
thrilled and fretting.

Gemma pacing the apron to throw
her hat, proud with flaws,
rotten with laughter;

Solvicha gazing into a window
cut through the backcloth
(piped birdsong);

Alma on the recliner, upstage,
gazing at the mounted gun
which will be used.

The Microwave

Those great domes built above reactors,
they now admit, were less nuclear science,
more safety features built with fingers crossed.

I've also heard at any chosen moment in London
there are more chicken wings than people,
frozen or frazzling or thrown to the pigeons.

The best ever wings were at The Virginian Hotel
in Medicine Bow, so crisp and toothsome
that my gourmet friend climbed down and took one.

A few miles out, Liberty I, the great wind turbine
strains on, its three wings spinning, frequent,
under turbulence and lightning, under avarice.

I've seen through forty, my life boiled down
to a glue of unexcitement or a stock of content,
depending on which way my mood is pointing.

Now, there are only things I already know
and things I do not need to: I might never explain
how the negative potential of the magnetron,

its resonating cavities bunching spiralling electrons,
makes a punnet of macaroni cheese bubble up,
softens a potato during the hourly headlines.

For decent spicy wings, buy some spicy wings,
spice them with cumin and paprika, glug some
soy sauce and mushroom ketchup. Zap them

for twice as long as they need, stirring once.
All my life I ran from trouble, from lovesome hands,
sharp fingers of power bringing nuclear dawn.

Bloom

You who thrived where the horse trod,
    where the apple smashed,
who shot up straight where the river sloshed
and rolled, who rose from blood;

    who ran your flag
up from the grifting dune
and pulled a pale sky down,
who budded on a sodden sack or log,

took seed and caught along the track's edge,
who jinked from crags and where walls slip,
    who broached the lip
of lintels, burst on finial and ledge;

you who tested luck and unluck,
thrift-fed, driven by wind and water,
    frost ticking each petal,
roping root and stem, the black

of black night lost to hope, you
cast the fine day as your fetch
and when it knocked and brought your wish
    and you were found, you grew.

To the End of the Day

Christopher, we have made a not quite prom scene,
gathered Kate Moss in your dress,
the ankle-length, the ruffled one the colour
of coffee ice cream, the not quite wild-side tower
of frills you sketched in sofa hours, skimming 80s flicks
for prairie snakeskin, drained workwear, bush duds

and there she struts and leans on a quayside piling
strung from chains, in the top-note
of the wind machine, nod-and-nudge raunch,
which half-drowns Quaife thumbing his bass
on 'Stop Your Sobbing', 'Set Me Free', a dress
to keep the chiffon mills of Italy thudding for seasons,

the Polaroid wall pinned with a dozen shots, her midnight
quarrel of attitudes, never in character,
the sum of distances from Dalston and Addiscombe,
Muswell Hill and Motherwell, to the not quite Christmas
weather hanging out on the side roads of NW10;
a dress of froth and strap, the milky tea dress, *that* dress.

Your Sunday Best

Counting on slender fingers, to comply
with your uncounted thoughts, dots of dust
in the morning, words lack mass,
abide as traces, patience not even a caveat.

Soon enough, girl, this porch will rot,
quick years surrender it to mulch and rust
as half-mile trains whistle by,
our patrons milky behind the inch-thick glass.

Church bells ring cold as they pass
but there is no wine, no bloom or must.
These boards will crack, but won't give yet.
Always fondly you defend me, unsure why.

Albemarle

So many times you'd been through it
and never once got off there: where people,
ever handsome, whistle as they step from the carriage,
strike out along the cream-bricked platform
swinging up their leather satchels.

Plush banks in the cutting lure rabbits
and day-flying moths, no foxes or flies, not one
junked mattress, no rusted tins of rail-lube. A station-master
up a ladder hangs bunting or freshens the blue
foot-high letters of ALBEMARLE.

The bridge above the tracks is painted
green and gold and beyond it children play late
in lush gardens. A guard waves from his hut as the rest of us
slump on, suddenly late, to the next grim station
and the smoggy hub of the city.

One day, you rise from your seat there,
unsure why, and a half-step through the doors,
some force musters in the calm and butts you back inside
and you roll in the aisle, clutching your guts,
aware it's no less than you deserve.

Against Confession

This suburban blogger parading her alarm,
bequeathing bitter smidgens of despair,
her tea-cup stormy full with bathtub gin,
will never set flames flooding, roaring
along the silver altar of the truth.

Nor this batsman, slogging lazy fours
into the damp edge, spitting bantam names
in Lenten twilight from beneath his tongue.
And the master knows still lifes still lie –
each skull and slipper orchid, each glazed sprat.

Stay calm. Stay quiet. Fever hasn't learned
its few bad lines. The knocking memories
inside your head are real enough – don't shake
them out, don't jam those polar jubilees
which stop you wading out into the sea.

Zodiac

These will be the signs of your cosmology:
the Octopod spooling in a slush of sea-stars,
the Chalice spilling drams of uptown chemistry,
the Catalogue of solemn asks and answers,
the Compass spinning in a lost man's grip,
an eye-sized Diamond swooning on a fist,
a rusting Coaster sailing on a map,
the Sweeper stooping to his trail of dust,
a Golden Eagle swooping on a mite,
the gamester Shoesmith swinging at his last,
a Skull and Crossbones serenading time,
the Stallion sucking at his block of salt,
two Turtles spooning in a cage of iron
under which, you claim, we'll be reborn.

The Damned

Kitten curious, or roaring down drinks
in Soho sumps, small hours tour buses,
satellite station green rooms, or conked

out in the bathtubs of motorway hotels,
there you were, with muckabout kisses,
sharking for the snappers, before hell

opened up for you and the weepy sores
of after-fame appeared, the haphazardry
and dwindling after three limelit years,

recognised with catcalls, wads of spit,
a nightclub fist, the scant camaraderie
melts fast, like your flat on Air Street,

the lhasa apso pups, the wraps and lines
of chang, the poster pull-outs, spray tan
smiles. It's paunch and palimony time

on Lucifer's leash. But for a madcap few
who cling, thin soup, one pillow Britain
is simmering with hatred, just for you.

Littoral

To the sandpiper, restlessly content
to run bedlam alongside her mate
on cacophonous stones or dip knee-deep
across sand flats, the churning foreshore

is all of real; she jolts onto a rock
but falling dizzy drops back into that
perpetual commotion of salt and bother
and with her beak conducts the sea.

Quietus

Where the brook runs to rust
and the torched charabancs lord the wheat
my shadow lengthens

And in the lanes and pits
of the parched city in the night's mid-night
my mood will quicken

And though not lost
my tongue will sicken for wine and wit
so long since tasted

The songs and slurs of cats
will jinx the air as I walk the limit
my third wish wasted

NOTES

Some of the poems were written using certain processes or are in forms I have developed. 'The Microkite' and 'The Microwave' are *hebdomads*, 'Jackpot', 'Shoreline Charismatic' and 'Bloom' are *charismatics*, 'Wetness as Motive Concept' and 'Contagious Light' are *relegated narratives*, 'A Story of Spice' and 'Your Sunday Best' are *overlays*. For details of these, see my website (www.vitamin-p.co.uk).

Against Complaint (11) is derived from the translation of a Yoruba poem ('Variety: why do we grumble') included in *The Penguin Book of Oral Poetry*, edited by R. Finnegan (1978).

Middleton (13) makes use of some material from a thread on 'worst towns and cities' on the music discussion forum Black Cat Bone.

DPD (16) is depersonalisation disorder.

A Story of Spice (19) is based on the opening paragraph of *Dangerous Tastes: The Story of Spices* (British Museum Press) by Andrew Dalby.

Warnerian (20) owes a debt to the style of the poet Ahren Warner.

Hunter's Stew (32) is a version of a short section of the 19th century epic *Pan Tadeusz* by Adam Mickiewicz.

Affinity (35) in one definition means a person with whom one has a natural bond. The word is derived from the Latin for 'to the boundary'.

Stone Tape Theory (39) is a scientific explanation of ghosts which suggests that minerals may store visual and aural information and later "replay" it.

Your Sunday Best (64) is based on a song of the same name by the US band Norfolk & Western.